DATE DUE

JUL 1 1 1992			
MAR 1 1993			
JUL 8 1993			
JUL 1 9 1993			
MAY 13 1999			
NOV 2 9 1999			
JUN 05 2003			
SEP 1 1 2003			
AUG 2 9 2012			
SEP 2 8 2016			

THIS OLD NEW HOUSE
Graham Learns About Renovating

Written and illustrated by
Sheila McGraw

Annick Press Ltd.

© 1989 Sheila McGraw
(Text and illustration)

Design and graphic realization
Sheila McGraw

Annick Press gratefully
acknowledges the support of
The Canada Council and the
Ontario Arts Council

**Canadian Cataloguing in
Publication Data**

McGraw, Sheila
This old new house: Graham
learns about renovating

ISBN 1-55037-035-9 (bound)
ISBN 1-55037-034-0 (pbk.)

1. Dwellings – Remodelling –
Juvenile literature.
I. Title.

TH4816.M34 1989   j690′.8′
0286   C88-094925-2

Distributed in Canada and the
USA by:
Firefly Books Ltd.,
250 Sparks Avenue
Willowdale, Ontario
M2H 2S4

Printed and bound in Canada
by D.W. Friesen & Sons Ltd.

To MAX AND GRAHAM

*Special thanks to Glen Anthony
for his help and expertise.*

The house next door to Graham's was old, run-down and dirty. No one had lived in it for many years. It was so ugly that Graham's father built a very high fence, so they wouldn't have to look at it.

One day, a FOR SALE sign appeared in front of the house. Rick and Sarah came, looked at the ugly, old house and bought it. They introduced themselves to Graham and his parents.

"We're going to *renovate*," said Rick.

"It's going to need a lot of work," Graham's Dad said. "I'm glad someone's going to fix it up."

"Me too," Graham said to himself.

"It will be beautiful when we're finished," Sarah said.

The next time they came over, Sarah and Rick had
Ms. Rollins with them. She was the *architect*. An architect
plans and designs buildings and houses. Ms. Rollins had rolls of
paper with her called *plans* and *blueprints*. Plans are the first
drawings the architect makes, and blueprints are copies that
are printed in blue and white. Ms. Rollins had made plans to
show where all the windows, doors, stairs, walls, and
everything would be that needs to be built. Plans are drawn to
scale, which is like taking the measurements of a building and
shrinking all of them by the same amount.

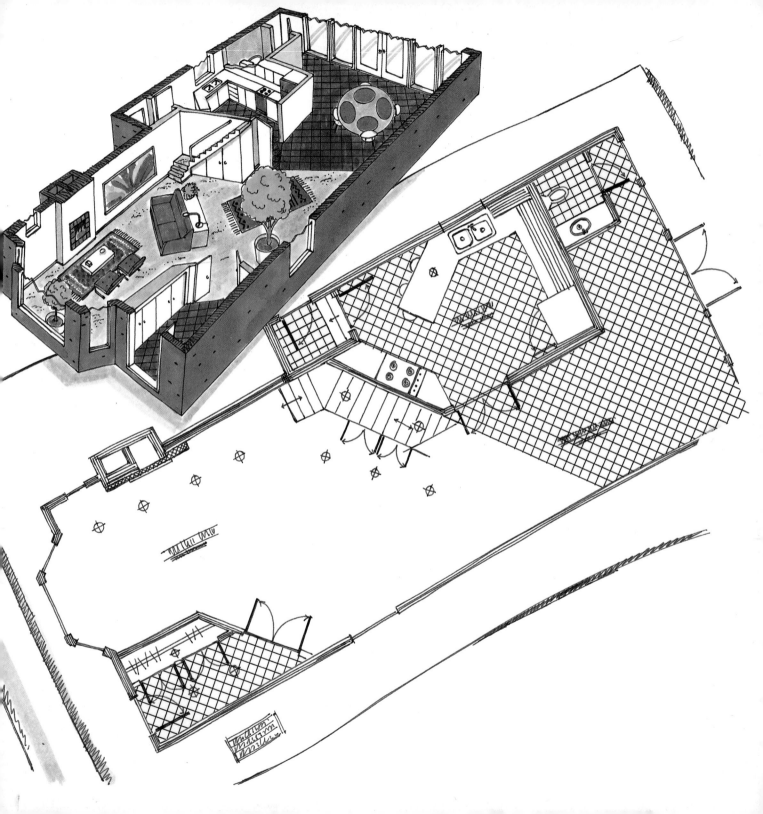

Sarah invited Graham to look inside the ugly, old house with them.

It was as bad inside as it was out. There was a narrow, dark entrance, big cracks in the walls and the whole place was dirty.

"Don't touch anything in here, Graham, you might catch a disease," Rick said with a laugh.

Everyone went down into the basement except Graham. There was a bad smell coming up the stairs and Graham got a shivery feeling.

"This place belongs in a horror movie," he thought, then he yelled, "Hey guys, I'm going home for dinner."

Ms. Rollins brought over the *permits* that she got from City Hall.

"Why do people need permits to build their houses?" Graham asked.

Ms. Rollins said, "Permits prove that people are doing their renovations properly. It would be nice if people could do whatever they wanted, but if there were no rules for building and renovating, people might build houses that are too crowded, unsafe, or unsuitable for their neighbourhood."

"What happens if you don't get permits?"

"Well, inspectors from the city come and check on your job, and they can make you stop building," Ms. Rollins said. She taped the permits to the windows.

The next day, George came to the house with several workers. He was the *contractor*. A contractor makes sure all the workers do their jobs properly, safely and on time. George let Graham try on his *safety gear,* and he said, "All the workers must wear hardhats in case anything falls on them, safety boots to protect their feet and safety goggles if they're doing something that might be dangerous to their eyes. Most workers wear protective gloves too."

A huge truck arrived and put a big metal *dumpster*, or bin, on the lawn. Five workers went into the house and smashed all the walls, ceilings and stairs, then threw all the pieces out the windows and into the bin. When the bin was full, the truck came back, dropped off an empty one and took the full one away.

Sarah, Rick and Graham went in to look around. It was very dirty and dusty in the house now. There were ladders instead of stairs, pieces of wood lying around and bare wires and pipes in the walls.

Sarah found an old newspaper with low prices for bread and eggs in the ads. Rick found some old pennies and a quarter.

All Graham found was a dried-up dead mouse.

"We'll keep everything but the mouse," Rick said.

It took a whole day to clean up a bit, then the *carpenters* started building the wall frames from long pieces of wood called *studs*, that are nailed together to form a kind of wall-skeleton. After the wall frames were built they could tell where the new walls would be.

The workers cut some new holes for the windows and covered them with plastic. They also cut holes in the floor where new stairs would go and they covered up the old stair holes with wood, so no one would fall through.

While the framing was going on inside, some men came and washed the grime off the brick outside and a *crew* from the city dug up the front yard to work on the water pipes.

Graham said, "Look at all the stuff down there!"

There were *sewers* that take dirty water away, pipes that bring clean water, *electrical cables, gas* and *telephone lines.* One of the workers explained to Graham what each was for, and he said, "The city is like a tree. A tree gets its life from its underground roots and the city gets its life from an underground system."

Graham phoned his friend Lillian to tell her about the men working underground and Lillian said, "There are also *subways* under some cities and some sewer pipes are so big, men can walk around in them."

Graham said, "George told me that rats live in some tunnels. Big ones with long skinny tails."

"E-e-w-w-w-w!" they both said.

The wall frames hold the *hidden services* for the house. One of these is *heating*. Most houses are heated with either gas or oil and some with electricity. Gas is carried in pipes from wells where it is taken from the ground. Oil is taken from the ground too, but it is delivered to your house by truck. Gas and oil are known as *fossil fuels*. Coal is a fossil fuel too.

The workers took out the big, old *furnace* and installed a new smaller one that won't use as much fuel, and that's important because if we use too much fossil fuel we might run out one day.

A strong fan in the furnace sucks cool air from all over the house down to the furnace, blows it over a fire to warm it up, then sends the warm air back to all the rooms through big square pipes called *ducts*. When you go out into the cold, you breathe in cold air, heat it in your body and blow out warm air, like a furnace.

"I can name all the appliances that run on *electricity*," Graham told George. "Toasters, vacuum cleaners, hairblowers, washers, dryers, refrigerators, clocks, televisions, computers, ovens, radios, blenders and freezers!"

"Hey! That's a long list. Don't forget though, that we also need electricity to run our furnaces and work our lights. It'd be dark and cold without electricity," George said.

"How does it work?" Graham asked.

George took off his hard hat and scratched his head. "Well," he said, "Electricity is a force, a power that you can't see. It travels inside cables that are strung along poles or run underground. From these, a wire goes into each house and into a metal box called an *electrical panel*. The *electricians* join lots of wires into the panel and install the wires through the walls of the house with switches and plugs along the way to plug appliances into and turn lights on and off."

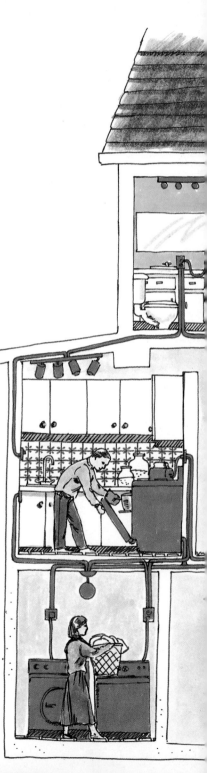

Rick and Sarah came to see their house nearly every day. Rick checked the wiring.

"It's really coming along," he said. "We'll be moving in a couple of weeks."

"Why are you moving?" Graham asked.

"We've always wanted to buy a house," Sarah explained. "We saved our money and decided that a house downtown was what we wanted most. We both like the feeling of history in the downtown area. A lot of the old houses and buildings have been torn down to build office towers and we're happy to help keep a bit of the city's history alive. The park with its big trees is really nice and we're also close to the museums, art galleries and shops that we like to go to."

Next the *plumber* came. "All our water comes from the lake," he told Graham.

"Yuk, lake water has *pollution* in it," Graham said.

The plumber laughed, "Don't worry, it all gets cleaned at the *filtration plant* before we get any. Then it's sent through *water mains* under the street and from there a pipe goes into your house, where it gets divided into hot and cold water pipes, with the hot water coming from a *water heater*. Those pipes go through the walls of the house to all the places where you need hot, cold and warm water."

"If all our clean water comes from the lake, where does all our dirty, used water go?" Graham asked.

The plumber chuckled, "Well, it goes back into the lake."

"Oh no!" Graham said, with a worried look.

"It's not as bad as it sounds," he said. "Our dirty water goes down *drains* into sewers which carry it to a *sewage treatment plant* where it's cleaned before it goes back into the lake.

George brought over a truckload of puffy, pink *fibreglass insulation*. The workers installed it in all the walls against the outside. They also put it in the roof and the basement. The insulation looked so cuddly that Graham wanted to jump on it.

"You can't play with insulation," George told him. "Fibreglass is made from glass that's spun into very thin threads. It's very itchy and the workers who install it wear heavy suits, gloves and hats to keep it off their skin. They also wear masks because it's dangerous to breathe the fibres into their lungs."

"Insulation keeps your house warm in the winter," Graham said. "I saw that in a commercial. It makes a *barrier* against the cold air."

"That's right," George said. "It also keeps your house cooler in the summer by keeping hot air out."

The insulation was the last thing to go into the walls, then they were all covered with *drywall* and painted.

Graham watched the long moving van pull up in front of the house. He carried the basket of cherries over that he had picked from the tree in his back yard, and placed it carefully on the porch out of the way of the movers. He went inside. There was soft carpet instead of plywood floors, a finished kitchen with new appliances, clean, new bathrooms, wooden stairways instead of ladders and a finished, un-smelly basement with a laundry room. "This place looks great," he thought.

Graham ran outside to greet Sarah and Rick who had arrived with their cat, Doodles. "Hey, this is an old house and a new house." Graham called, "An old new house!"

"That's right," Rick said, holding the cat. "And we've got our old friend Doodles and our new friend Graham."

Sarah and Rick both gave Graham a big hug.

GLOSSARY

ARCHITECT A person who designs buildings.

BARRIER An obstacle. Insulation prevents air from getting through.

BLUEPRINT A copy of plans, printed in blue.

CARPENTERS People who work with wood.

CONTRACTOR A person who oversees the work of building, after plans are made.

CREW A group of workers.

DRAINS Pipes that carry away water or sewage to large sewers.

DRYWALL Ready-made plaster boards to close in or cover, walls or framing.

DUCTS Tubes or pipes to carry air for heating. Ducts can also carry gas or cables.

DUMPSTER (Slang) A large metal bin to collect rubbish.

ELECTRICAL CABLES Bundles of insulated wires that carry electricity.

ELECTRICAL PANEL A metal box where the electrical wires of a house join the main cable from the street.

ELECTRICIANS People who install wires and work with electricity.

ELECTRICITY An invisible form of energy that travels in a current, through metal wires.

FIBREGLASS Threads of glass, pressed to form insulation, or woven for other uses.

FILTRATION PLANT A building where water is filtered to remove dirt and other particles.

FOSSIL FUEL Oil, gas or coal, which we use for fuel, formed in the earth thousands of years ago.

FURNACE An apparatus which heats a house or building.

GAS LINES Pipes that carry natural gas to homes and buildings for heating.

HEATING A method of warming a house.

HIDDEN SERVICES The equipment, hidden in the walls, that makes services like heating, plumbing, electricity, etc. work.

INSULATION A barrier against either warm air in the summer, or cold air in the winter.

PERMITS Written permission from City Hall to build or renovate to approved plans.

PLAN Drawing that shows a floor of a building, drawn to scale.

PLUMBER A person who installs or works with water pipes and drains.

POLLUTION Dirt that contaminates or poisons the earth, water or air.

RENOVATE To repair, update or beautify an old or neglected house or building.

SAFETY GEAR Protective clothing worn to prevent injury in the work place.

SCALE Drawings shrunk uniformly and in proportion to their surroundings.

SEWAGE TREATMENT PLANT A building where water from sewers is cleaned and disinfected before entering lakes or rivers.

SEWER An underground pipe or channel to carry off sewage or rainwater.

STUDS The wooden framework inside a wall.

SUBWAY An underground railway.

TELEPHONE LINES Cables or wires that carry signals, either strung along poles or buried underground.

WATER HEATER An insulated metal tank that heats and stores hot water.

WATER MAIN A main pipe or channel for carrying clean water to houses and buildings.